Social Media Mastery: Grow Your Online Presence

Fritz J. Ballard

Acknowledgments

The process of writing this book, which is titled "Embracing the Future of Social Media," has been an amazing adventure that has been full of learning in addition to exploration and creativity. For the realization of this project, I would like to extend my most sincere gratitude to each and every person who contributed to its success.

First and foremost, I would want to express my deepest gratitude to my family for their unflinching support, encouragement, and understanding throughout the entire process of writing. You have been my guiding light, providing me with the inspiration to pursue my passion and share my thoughts with the world. Thank you for your love and encouragement.

The essential knowledge, expertise, and encouragement that I received from my mentor and advisors is something for which I am extremely grateful. Both the substance of this book and my grasp of the intricate and ever-changing environment of social media have been significantly influenced by your wisdom and insights, which have been important in molding the content of this book.

It is with deep gratitude that I express my appreciation to the staff at the publishing house for their expertise, devotion, and assistance in the process of bringing this book into existence. The transformation of thoughts into words and words into an actual reality has been greatly aided by your creative abilities, competence, and meticulous attention to detail.

Regarding the substance of this book, I would like to express my profound gratitude to the innumerable individuals and organizations whose efforts and contributions have influenced and inspired the content. Your forward-thinking thoughts, ground-breaking research, and thought-provoking insights have contributed to the enhancement of the story and broadened the scope of my comprehension.

Lastly, but certainly not least, I would want to express my deepest gratitude to all of the readers who have joined me on this journey. You are the driving force behind this attempt, and it is my honest hope that this book will inspire and encourage you to embrace the future of social media with confidence and creativity. Your interest, passion, and involvement are the driving force behind this work.

© [2024] [Fritz J. Ballard]. All rights reserved.

Without the prior written permission of the publisher, no portion of this publication may be reproduced, distributed, or transmitted in any form or by any means, including photocopying, recording, or other electronic or mechanical methods. The only exceptions to this rule are brief quotations that are incorporated into critical reviews and certain other noncommercial uses that are permitted by copyright law.

CONTENT

Chapters:

INTRODUCTION 9

Understanding the Landscape of Social Media 13

Setting Your Social Media Goals 18

Crafting Compelling Content Strategies 25

Leveraging Visuals for Maximum Impact 30

Engaging with Your Audience Effectively 35

Harnessing the Power of Hashtags 40

Navigating Algorithm Changes and Trends 46

Building a Strong Personal Brand 51

Collaborating with Influencers and Partners 56

Analyzing Metrics and Data for Success 62

Handling Negative Feedback and Crisis Management 68

Scaling Your Social Media Presence 73

Exploring Emerging Platforms and Trends 78

Monetizing Your Social Media Following 83

Sustaining Long-Term Growth and Success 89

INRODUCTION:

Social media is a tremendous force in today's interconnected society, where digital landscapes affect our daily interactions and influence our decisions. In this context, social media is particularly influential. It is not only a platform for sharing images or interacting with friends; rather, it is a dynamic ecosystem that facilitates the growth of enterprises, molds opinions, and accelerates careers. Mastering social media is not merely a desirable skill; rather, it is an absolute requirement. This is true whether you are an experienced marketer who is attempting to navigate the complexity of online advertising or an aspiring influencer who is looking to carve out a space for yourself in the digital sphere.

We would like to take this opportunity to welcome you to a thorough guide that will help you understand the complexities of social media and provide you with the skills and techniques you need to survive in this always shifting environment. This book is your guide to unlocking the full potential of social media, from grasping the subtleties of different platforms to writing interesting content that resonates with your audience. It is your roadmap to maximizing the potential of social media.

Following this, we will begin on a voyage into the diverse

world of social media, examining its numerous facets and learning the secrets to developing a powerful online presence. This adventure will take place in the pages that follow. You can find something here that will be useful to you, regardless of whether you are a rookie trying to find your way through the maze of hashtags and algorithms or an experienced professional looking to improve your technique.

As we go on this trip, the first thing we need to do is have a knowledge of the underlying ideas that comprise social networking. In this session, we will investigate the psychological aspects of user engagement, specifically focusing on the variables that motivate individuals to like, share, and comment on content. Through the process of gaining insights into the behaviors and motives of your audience, you will be better positioned to personalize your content and maximize the impact it has.

Following that, we will go into the art of producing captivating material that not only captures attention but also motivates people to take action. In this lesson, we will discuss the components that contribute to the success of storytelling in the digital age, including intriguing captions and visually appealing content. We will offer you with the tools and techniques that will enable you to make your content stand out in the competitive online scene, whether you are creating videos for YouTube, curating photographs for Instagram, or drafting tweets for Twitter.

But mastering social media isn't only about producing excellent content; it's also about cultivating meaningful relationships with the people who follow you on social media. For the purpose of establishing trust and loyalty that extends beyond the sphere of digital media, we will demonstrate how to cultivate genuine ties with your followers. We are going to discuss the numerous ways in which you can create a dedicated fanbase and foster a sense of community. These include responding to comments and messages, having live question and answer sessions, and conducting interactive polls.

The significance of data-driven insights is, of course, something that must be brought up in any conversation about social media in order to be considered comprehensive. We are going to demonstrate how to make use of the power of analytics in order to monitor your performance, evaluate your achievements, and make adjustments to your strategy. Through the utilization of data to guide your decision-making process, you will be able to fine-tune your strategy and produce even more impressive outcomes.

Throughout the entirety of this journey, each chapter is intended to present you with concrete insights and straightforward advice that you can immediately put into practice. In this book, you will find the definitive guide to achieving success in the digital era, regardless of whether you are just beginning your social media journey or are ready to take your game to the next level.

To put it another way, are you prepared to release the full power of social media and revolutionize your presence on the internet? The skills and methods that are presented in this book will enable you to achieve your goals, regardless of whether you are an entrepreneur who wants to develop your business, an influencer who wants to increase your reach, or a marketer who wants to stay ahead of the curve. Together, let's plunge in and start this trip that will change our lives profoundly.

Chapter 1: Understanding the Landscape of Social Media

The way in which we engage with one another, share information, and take in content has been revolutionized by social media, which has become an indispensable component of our everyday lives. The purpose of this chapter is to begin on a trip to study the multidimensional world of social media platforms. These platforms range from the behemoths such as Facebook, Instagram, and Twitter to niche platforms that are customized to specific interests and demographics.

Facebook, a social networking giant that boasts more than 2.8 billion monthly active members, is poised to be at the vanguard of this digital revolution. Because of its unrivaled reach and advanced targeting capabilities, it is a formidable tool for companies and advertisers who are looking to engage with the consumers they are trying to reach. Facebook Pages, Groups, and Ads are some of the tools that allow brands to interact with people in a variety of different ways, which helps to cultivate communities and drive conversions.

The social media network Instagram, which was purchased by Facebook in 2012, has become the most prominent medium for visual storytelling. Instagram has evolved into a playground for both marketers and influencers for the simple reason that it places a strong focus on visually attractive material and short-form video content. The dynamic elements of the platform, like as Stories, Reels, and IGTV, give users the ability to express their creativity and authenticity, which in turn makes it easier for them to create meaningful connections with their followers.

Twitter, which is distinguished by its rapid-fire and succinct format, functions as a central location for real-time information, where conversations and breaking news simultaneously take place. Because of its low character capacity, it emphasizes brevity and wit, which makes it a fertile field for content that goes viral and to themes that are currently trending. Twitter allows companies to interact with their target audience, offer assistance to their customers, and take part in cultural conversations, all of which contribute to an increase in their reach and significance.

LinkedIn, on the other hand, is geared at providing services to professionals and has positioned itself as the most prominent platform for business-to-business marketing, recruitment, and networking. LinkedIn, which has more than 700 million users, provides professionals with chances that are unmatched in terms of showcasing their knowledge, establishing important connections, and expanding their professional networks. Within the context of the business world, LinkedIn acts as a central location for thought leadership, the creation of leads, and the awareness of brands.

The landscape of social media extends beyond these titans, comprising a multitude of platforms that cater to certain demographics and interests in a niche market. Through its short-form video format, TikTok has managed to engage audiences of Generation Z all over the world. TikTok is widely regarded as the platform that gave rise to viral dance challenges and funny sketches. By utilizing TikTok's sophisticated algorithm and engaging content forms, brands are able to interact with younger populations in ways that are both genuine and innovative.

Snapchat, which is well-known for its ephemeral messaging and augmented reality features, provides a one-of-a-kind platform for companies to interact with younger consumers in ways that are both playful and engaging. Brands are able to create memorable experiences that resonate with Snapchat's user base thanks to the innovative advertising possibilities that Snapchat provides, such as sponsored lenses and geofilters.

Pinterest, which places an emphasis on visual discovery and inspiration, functions as a virtual pinboard that offers users the opportunity to collect ideas for a variety of topics, including fashion, home design, and cuisine. By utilizing Pinterest's visual search features and rich Pins, brands are able to showcase their items and inspire visitors, ultimately resulting in increased traffic and conversions.

The landscape of social media is always shifting, and at the same time, new platforms are being developed and current ones are adjusting to accommodate shifting user tastes and habits. Clubhouse, an audio-based social network that is redefining live discussions, and Twitch, a live streaming platform that is dominating the gaming and esports industry, are two examples of how innovation thrives in the digital age.

Individuals and businesses alike must make it a priority to be current on these advancements and to have a thorough awareness of the subtleties that are associated with each platform. It is possible for businesses to develop bespoke strategies that resonate with their target demographics by exploiting the distinctive characteristics and audiences of various platforms. This will ultimately lead to more engagement and loyalty, which will ultimately lead to increased business growth.

We are going to go deeper into tactics for enhancing your presence on each platform in the next chapters. We are going to harness the power of social media in order to accomplish your objectives more effectively. Now is the time to strap your seatbelt and be ready to traverse the ever-evolving and dynamic terrain of social media with self-assurance and knowledge.

Chapter 2: Setting Your Social Media Goals

Establishing goals that are both lucid and measurable is an essential step to take before digging further into the enormous expanse of social media channels. It is possible that your efforts on social platforms will not be coherent and will not produce the outcomes that you envision if you do not have a clear direction to follow.

Do some self-reflection and ask yourself, "What do I want to achieve through the use of social media?" Your aims should be in perfect harmony with your larger business goals, whether they involve increasing the visibility of your brand, directing traffic to your website, cultivating prospects, or increasing sales.

Having identified your objectives, the next step is to ensure that they are SMART, which stands for specific, measurable, attainable, relevant, and time-bound at the same time. Consider the following example: rather than setting a vague objective such as "increase followers," you should aim to achieve a particular quantity of new followers within a predetermined amount of time.

The next step is to break down your overarching goals into more manageable, specific targets. To give you an example, if you want to increase engagement, you may set goals that are tied to metrics such as the number of likes, comments, shares, and click-through rates.

When you have your goals and objectives in hand, you are now in a position to develop a plan that is specific to each social media platform. Because different platforms serve a variety of functions and are geared toward different demographics, it is necessary to develop a strategy that is specific to each platform.

As an illustration, if you want to increase the amount of traffic that visits your website, you may concentrate on publishing blog entries, product updates, and exclusive deals on social media sites such as Facebook and Twitter respectively. Platforms such as Instagram and Pinterest, on the other hand, would be more suitable paths to pursue if your purpose is to exhibit the visual identity of your brand.

The process of goal-setting is an iterative one that requires periodic assessment and recalibration. It is essential to keep in mind that goal-setting is not a one-time event that can be completed and then forgotten about. As you progress through your social media journey and gain insights from analytics, you should be ready to adjust your objectives and approach in accordance with the new information you obtain.

You will not only be able to maintain your motivation and clarity if you define goals that are both clear and attainable, but you will also be able to evaluate your progress and evaluate your level of success over time. Consequently, it is essential to devote some of your time and energy to the process of outlining your objectives, as this is the fundamental cornerstone of social media mastery.

In the current environment, which is driven by digital technology, social media has grown to become an indispensable instrument for individuals and businesses alike to connect with, engage with, and conduct business with their audience. Nevertheless, in the midst of the huge ocean of platforms, trends, and strategies, it is simple to lose sight of one essential component, which is the establishment of goals that are both specific and attainable.

A road plan, a guiding light in the middle of the turbulent waves of social media, can be obtained through the process of goal setting. It provides a sense of direction to your efforts, making certain that each and every post, interaction, and campaign is both purposeful and in line with the larger goals that you have set for yourself.

But what are the factors that contribute to the success of a goal? The following are the basic characteristics of a well-crafted objective, which are encapsulated in the acronym SMART:

specified : A objective that is specified is entirely transparent and devoid of any ambiguity. The statement does not provide for any opportunity for interpretation or misunderstanding. Instead of settling for a general objective such as "increase engagement," you should go for a more specific target such as "increase Instagram engagement by 20% within three months."

Measurable: Measurability is essential for defining success and evaluating progress in a course of action. You are able to track your performance in an objective manner if you have a measurable goal because it is quantifiable. If you want to track the growth of your followers, the traffic to your website, or the conversion rates, you need make sure that your goals are quantifiable.

Achievable : While it is essential to have lofty objectives, it is also essential to establish objectives that are within one's attainment. A goal that is attainable is one that is both reasonable and practicable, taking into consideration elements such as resources, time, and experience. Setting objectives that are impossible to achieve can result in feelings of dissatisfaction and demotivation, which can undermine your efforts.

In the context of your business or activity, a relevant aim is one that is in line with your more general objectives and makes a contribution to the overall success of the endeavor or enterprise. You should ask yourself, "Does this goal align with my business priorities?" before you set a goal for yourself. Are they relevant to the people I'm trying to reach? Your efforts will be more concentrated and have a greater impact if you guarantee that they are relevant.

The establishing of a deadline instills a sense of urgency and accountability, which is important because time is a valuable commodity. When a goal is time-bound, it is specified that it must be accomplished within a certain amount of time, which provides a sense of direction and momentum. Setting deadlines, whether they are weekly, monthly, or quarterly, encourages productivity and progress. This is true regardless of the aim.

Following the creation of SMART goals, the subsequent stage is to transform those goals into targets that may be actively pursued. All of these are the stepping stones that will help you bridge the gap between your long-term objectives and the activities you engage in on social media on a daily basis.

As an illustration, if you want to raise people's knowledge of your brand, some of your aims could include the following:

- Within the next six months, increase the number of followers by twenty percent.
Using social media efforts, generate one hundred new leads every single day.
Achieve a thirty percent increase in website traffic via social media within a period of three months.

The accomplishment of each target serves as a milestone, directing your efforts and offering a concrete indicator of your progress. You will be able to ensure consistent progress and keep your focus in spite of the always shifting landscape of social media if you break down your goals into smaller, more manageable tasks.

For the purpose of achieving success on social media, it is essential to establish goals that are both specific and attainable. Your efforts will be provided with direction, clarity, and purpose as a result of this, and it will ensure that each and every activity contributes to the accomplishment of your more comprehensive goals. By adhering to the SMART framework and breaking down your goals into actionable targets, you will be able to negotiate the complexity of social media with self-assurance and a sense of purpose. It is also important to take the time to carefully outline your objectives, since they serve as the road map to achieving mastery of social media.

Chapter 3: Crafting Compelling Content Strategies

In the frenetic world of social media, where each scroll brings up a fresh opportunity for engagement, content is the foundation around which connections are built. In the middle of the cacophony of voices competing for attention, it is the currency that can be used to buy attention, develop relationships, and foster community. But how does one traverse this sea of competing narratives and make sure that their material emerges as a beacon of resonance for the audience that they are trying to reach? The answer can be found in the skill of developing compelling content strategies that speak directly to the minds, hearts, and aspirations of the people you are trying to engage.

1. **Know Your Audience:**

Before setting out on the path of content production, it is absolutely necessary to go on a journey of comprehension. Learn as much as you can about the demographics, hobbies, and problems that are experienced by the audience. In what ways do they function? What causes them to stay awake at night? You may forge a relationship that goes beyond simple interaction by carefully developing audience personas. This will allow you to personalize your content to address the individual requirements and desires of your audience.

2. Share your personal narrative:
In a sea of sponsored content, the human touch is the one that resonates the most deeply with potential customers. Storytelling possesses a special ability to fascinate, connect, and motivate people to take action. Storytelling empowers your brand by imbuing it with depth, authenticity, and relatability. This can be accomplished through the use of behind-the-scenes glances, client testimonials, or personal experiences. The stories that we tell are the ones that leave a long-lasting impression on the hearts of our audience, which is especially important in a world when sales pitches are everywhere.

3. In addition to engaging the audience:
When it comes down to it, content is a fine balance between providing value and entertaining the audience. You should educate your audience by providing them with articles that are insightful, guidelines that are comprehensive, and tutorials that are step-by-step. This will enable them to overcome problems and broaden their perspectives. In addition, incorporate aspects of entertainment into your content. This

can be accomplished through the use of attractive imagery, humorous anecdotes, or interactive experiences that pique the audience's interest and encourage participation.

Accept and Embrace Visuals Four:
Visuals are the lifeblood of engagement in a digital universe that is governed by attention spans that are ephemeral. Consider making an investment in engaging pictures, intriguing films, and eye-catching infographics that not only attract attention but also effectively communicate your message in a way that is both clear and impactful. Your information can be elevated to a higher level and leave a lasting impact on your audience through the use of visuals, which can be accomplished through the use of breathtaking photography or exciting motion graphics.

Be Consistent: the fifth point
Throughout the turbulent waves of social media, consistency serves as the lighthouse that guides your audience through the maze of information. In order to ensure that your audience is aware of your brand at all times, you should create a content calendar and stick to a regular posting schedule. Whether you publish once a day, once a week, or twice a week, maintaining a consistent posting schedule can help you build familiarity, dependability, and trust, which are the foundations of a strong

social media presence.

Sixth, Encourage Participation:
Rather than only serving as a medium for communication and engagement, social media platforms can serve as a platform for broadcasting. Whether it be through likes, comments, shares, or tags, encourage your audience to actively participate in the conversation by encouraging them to contribute. In order to cultivate a sense of community and belonging in relation to your business, you should ask questions that provoke thought, conduct surveys that need participation, and start meaningful conversations.

It is important to optimize for each platform.
Different social media platforms each have their own particular quirks and peculiarities that are unique to them. Make sure that your material is tailored to the structure and tone of each network, whether it be the brief wit of Twitter, the visual magnificence of Instagram, or the professional attitude of LinkedIn. Through the process of optimizing your content for each platform, you are able to increase its reach, resonance, and effect, so ensuring that it will resonate with your audience regardless of where they may be browsing.

In conclusion, the process of developing appealing content

strategies is a combination of art and science. It is a delicate tango between creativity and strategy, while also involving empathy and statistics. You are able to generate content that not only attracts attention but also cultivates genuine connections, drives engagement, and ultimately accomplishes your social media goals if you have an understanding of your audience, embrace the art of storytelling, and give value in a consistent and authentic manner. Now is the time to set sail on the limitless sea of social media, armed with the power of captivating content, and allow your tale to unfold across the digital horizon.

Chapter 4: Leveraging Visuals for Maximum Impact

When it comes to brands that want to create an effect on social media, the strategic use of graphics has become very necessary in today's fast-paced digital landscape, where attention spans are short and competition for eyeballs is severe. We are going to delve into the complexities of properly utilizing graphics in order to attract attention, communicate brand messaging, and drive engagement in this chapter.

1. Quality Over Quantity:

When there is an abundance of content in a congested environment, quality is the most important factor. Make an investment in high-resolution photographs and films that have been made by professionals. These should not only represent your business but also inspire your audience to connect with it. In addition to leaving an unfavorable impression, graphics that are pixelated or blurry might distract from the quality of your message. In order to distinguish your brand from the competition and demonstrate your dedication to excellence, you should make quality your top priority.

2. Show, Don't Tell:

The potential of visuals to transmit feelings and thoughts that are difficult to understand in a single instant is singular. Instead of depending exclusively on text to express the value proposition of your brand, you should make use of visually attractive photographs and videos to display the benefits of your product, emphasize testimonials from satisfied customers, and showcase the personality of your brand. Because you are showing rather than explaining, you are able to provide your audience with an experience that is more immersive and unforgettable.

Create a Branding Strategy That Is Consistent:
When it comes to establishing trust with your audience and generating brand recognition, consistency is really essential. You should work on developing a visual identity that is consistent across all social media channels and that embodies the personality, values, and aesthetic of your brand. When you want to create a unified brand experience that resonates with your audience and promotes the identity of your brand at every touchpoint, you should use colors, fonts, and imagery that are consistent with one another.

Experiment using a variety of different formats because:
In order to maintain the freshness and interest of your material,

you should embrace creativity and experiment with a variety of graphic layouts. Each format provides a different set of options to engage your audience and convey the story of your brand in an engaging manner. These opportunities range from static images and GIFs to carousel posts and live videos of your brand. This allows you to appeal to a variety of preferences and attract the attention of a larger audience. Diversifying your visual content is one way to accomplish this.

5. Optimize based on mobile devices:
Due to the fact that the majority of people who use social media platforms reach them through mobile devices, it is absolutely necessary to optimize your visuals for mobile viewing. It is important to ensure that your images and videos load quickly, that your content is succinct and understandable, and that you make use of thumbnails that are appealing to the eye in order to give a smooth user experience on mobile devices. Putting mobile optimization at the forefront of your priorities allows you to effectively communicate with and engage with your audience across all devices.

Take Advantage of Content Generated by Users:
User-generated material, also known as UGC, presents a significant opportunity for companies to establish credibility and individuality online. In order to showcase user-generated

content (UGC) on your social media channels, you should encourage your audience to share their experiences with purchasing your products or services. This not only serves to validate and provide social evidence, but it also helps to cultivate a sense of community and belonging among the people who follow you through social media. You are able to humanize your brand and strengthen connections with your audience by utilizing user-generated content (UGC).

The seventh step is to monitor performance and iterate:
For a visual content strategy to be effective, it is necessary to continuously evaluate and iterate depending on performance data. For the purpose of determining how effective your images are, you should make use of analytics to monitor important metrics such as engagement rates, click-through rates, and conversion rates. In order to improve your visual strategy and produce content that resonates with your audience, it is important to recognize patterns and trends in the data that tracks performance. You may optimize your visual material for maximum effect and produce real outcomes on social media by taking a data-driven strategy. This technique allows you to tailor your content.

In conclusion, the strategic use of visuals is essential for brands seeking to stand out and succeed in today's competitive social media landscape. When organizations put quality, originality, consistency, and optimization at the forefront of their visual strategy, they are able to effectively employ images to attract attention, communicate brand messages, and drive engagement. Brands have the ability to improve their online presence and establish stronger connections with their audience by embracing the power of graphics, which ultimately leads to long-term success in the digital realm.

Chapter 5: Engaging with Your Audience Effectively

When it comes to the ever-changing environment of social media, successful interaction with your audience is not merely a tactic; rather, it is an essential component for achieving success. In addition to simply disseminating your message, the most important thing is to cultivate true connections and relationships with the people who follow you. In the following chapter, we will delve into crucial methods that will allow you to effectively engage with your audience, cultivate loyalty, and drive long-term success on social media platforms.

Make sure you are responsive:

The importance of being sensitive to the comments, messages, and mentions made by your audience cannot be overstated. You can demonstrate your dedication to meeting the requirements of your audience by promptly responding to their questions, concerns, or feedback. When you participate fully in talks, you not only demonstrate your appreciation for their participation, but you also develop trust and credibility to the other person. Remember that prompt reactions can make all the difference in the world when it comes to developing a devoted following.

The second step is to start conversations:
Rather than waiting for your audience to start talks, you should take the initiative to generate conversations between them. Encourage conversations that are pertinent to your brand by asking questions that provoke thought, soliciting comments, or posing inquiries. Creating an environment that is welcoming and inclusive, in which your audience feels respected and heard, can be accomplished by starting conversations. This preventative strategy helps to cultivate a feeling of community and invigorates the connection that exists between your brand and the people who follow it.

Personalize your interactions by doing the following:
It is of the utmost importance to treat your audience as active participants rather than merely as bystanders. In order to personalize your interactions with people, you should address them by their name, acknowledge the interests they have, and adjust your responses to the specific requirements they have. Through the demonstration of genuine interest and empathy, you are able to establish significant connections that resonate with your audience on a personal level. Through the use of this individualized strategy, loyalty is fostered, and continuing involvement is encouraged.

Encourage user-generated content (UGC) by saying the following:

Through the encouragement of user-generated content, you can provide your audience the ability to become co-creators of the story of your brand. Request that they share their experiences, photographs, and testimonials that are associated with the items or services that you offer. Not only does user-generated content (UGC) give genuine content, but it also develops a sense of community and belonging among the people who follow you. Displaying content that was developed by users is a great way to show thanks for the contributions made by your audience and to enhance their devotion to those efforts.

5. Organize Question and Answer Sessions and Live Streams:

When you organize live question-and-answer sessions and live streaming, you provide yourself with great possibilities to engage with your audience in real time. Motivate customers to engage in conversations about issues that are pertinent to your brand by asking questions, sharing ideas, and participating in discussions. Your brand will become more approachable and relatable as a result of these engaging sessions, which will also humanize it. Establishing trust and developing deeper connections with your audience can be accomplished through the promotion of open communication.

(6) Demonstrate your gratitude by:
Demonstrating appreciation for the support and participation of your audience is a crucial component in the process of cultivating strong relationships. You should make an effort to express gratitude to them for their comments, shares, or participation in the debates. Additionally, as a sign of thanks, you might think about providing special discounts or perks. You can develop a network of devoted brand advocates and reinforce the value of their engagement by demonstrating genuine appreciation for their continued participation.

Monitoring Conversations and Emotions is the Seventh Step:
Keeping a close eye on the conversations that are taking place around your business is really necessary in order to comprehend the feelings and perspectives of your audience. In order to keep track of mentions, hashtags, and keywords that are associated with your brand and industry, you need make use of social listening tools. It is important to pay great attention to both positive and negative input, and to reply quickly in order to address any concerns or problems that may

arise. Taking an active role in monitoring conversations demonstrates both your responsiveness and your dedication to ensuring the satisfaction of your customers.

To summarize, the foundation of a successful social media strategy is building a strong relationship with your audience through effective participation. Your ability to create a devoted following and foster meaningful connections with your audience can be enhanced by placing an emphasis on responsiveness, initiating conversations, personalizing interactions, and encouraging user-generated material. Furthermore, by organizing live sessions, demonstrating appreciation, and monitoring interactions, you are able to modify and improve your strategy based on feedback received in real time. In the end, if you place a high value on interaction, you will be able to cultivate a healthy community of brand advocates who will promote your brand to others, which will ultimately lead to sustainable development and success on social media platforms.

Chapter 6: Harnessing the Power of Hashtags

For the purpose of increasing visibility, stimulating interaction, and connecting communities, hashtags have evolved as significant tools in the modern digital age, which is characterized by the dominance of social media platforms as centers of communication and content consumption. Gaining an understanding of how to make good use of hashtags can have a big impact on the success of your efforts to manage your social media accounts. Within this chapter, we delve into the complexities of hashtag strategy, providing you with insights and strategies that you can put into practice to assist you in navigating the ever-changing world of social media with ease.

1. Research Relevant Hashtags:

Prior to beginning your journey with hashtags, it is essential to begin by conducting extensive research in order to locate hashtags that are relevant to your specific business or specialty. Exploring trending hashtags, determining their popularity, and determining whether or not they are relevant to your target audience can be accomplished with the use of programs such as Hashtagify, RiteTag, and Trendsmap. For the purpose of optimizing your social media presence and attracting the appropriate audience, you should connect your hashtags with the identity of your business and the subjects of your content.

2. Generate Unique Hashtags for Your Brand:

In addition to making use of hashtags that are already in use, you should also think about creating branded hashtags that are specific to your business or campaign. Hashtags that are associated with your brand can act as one-of-a-kind identifiers, allowing your content to stand out in the competitive social media scene. Not only can they increase brand recognition, but they also encourage user-generated content, which helps to cultivate a feeling of community among your audience. If you want your branded hashtags to be as effective as possible, you should make sure they are easy to remember, simple to spell, and reflect the values that your company stands for.

3. Make Use of a Combination of General and Specific Hashtags:

When it comes to improving your reach and engagement, one of the most important things you can do is find a balance between niche-specific hashtags and wide, popular hashtags. To increase the visibility of your material, you should use broad hashtags like #instagood or #photooftheday. These hashtags appeal to a large audience. On the other hand, niche hashtags such as #veganrecipes or #digitalnomadlife make it possible for you to target a more specific audience that is enthusiastic about the themes that you are specializing in. Through the utilization of a wide variety of hashtags in your posts, you have the ability to extend your reach while preserving your relevance to the audience you are trying to capture.

Fourth, make sure that your hashtags are relevant and contextual:

Although hashtags have the potential to increase discoverability, it is crucial to make sure that they continue to be relevant and contextual to the material you are sharing. You should steer clear of using generic hashtags since they water down the meaning of your article. Instead, you should choose hashtags that are relevant to the interests of your audience. Maintaining a natural flow and improving readability can be accomplished by incorporating hashtags into your captions or comments in a seamless environment. You can effectively engage your audience and promote meaningful interactions by ensuring that your hashtags are used in a manner that is consistent with the material you provide.

5. Gain an Advantage by Utilizing Popular Hashtags:

Monitoring hashtags that are currently trending provides an opportunity to capitalize on conversations that are related to your brand and increase your visibility. The use of discretion, on the other hand, is absolutely necessary in order to avoid giving the impression of being opportunistic or out of touch with your brand identity. Make sure that your engagement in popular subjects is in line with the values and voice of your company. This will ensure that you are authentic and relevant. You may increase your reach and engagement by strategically including trending hashtags into your content. This will allow you to capitalize on the momentum of hot debates within your audience.

Experiment with different hashtag strategies, number six:

Consider adopting an attitude of experimentation in order to improve the effectiveness of your hashtag strategy and reach your goals. Experiment with various hashtag combinations, adjusting the quantity of hashtags used in each post, and evaluate the impact of these combinations using analytics tools. By monitoring metrics such as engagement rate and reach, you will be able to determine which hashtags are most popular with your audience and adjust your strategy appropriately. Your ability to remain ahead of trends and optimize your influence on social media may be achieved by continuously iterating and adjusting your hashtag approach.

Participate in Hashtag Communities: The Seventh Step

Going beyond the simple act of using hashtags, actively connecting with groups that are associated with hashtags can result in significant benefits for your company. It is important to take part in conversations that are pertinent, to interact with posts that contain relevant hashtags, and to produce content that is beneficial to the community. Through the cultivation of genuine connections and the provision of contributions that are of significant value, you can establish yourself as a respected authority within your preferred field. The cultivation of relationships inside hashtag communities results in the development of a devoted following, the promotion of organic growth, and an increase in the legitimacy of your business.

In conclusion, leveraging the power of hashtags takes more than just the use of tokens; it calls for a strategic approach that is founded on research, innovation, and involvement with the community. Increasing your social media presence, amplifying your message, and establishing meaningful connections with your target audience are all possible outcomes that may be achieved through the thorough curation of your hashtag strategy. When you are navigating the ever-changing landscape of social media, it is important to keep in mind that hashtags are more than simply symbols; they are doorways to opportunities that will allow you to accomplish your objectives and leave an indelible mark in the space of digital communication.

Chapter 7: Navigating Algorithm Changes and Trends

When it comes to the fast-paced world of social media, where algorithms are the most important thing, it is of the utmost importance for individuals and brands alike to be able to adjust to changes and ahead of trends. By gaining a knowledge of and making use of these changes, you can substantially impact both your reach and engagement. This is because platforms are constantly working to improve their algorithms in order to provide consumers with the most relevant information. In this chapter, we will discuss various tactics that can be utilized to efficiently navigate algorithmic changes and trends.

1. Stay Informed:

It is necessary to have a proactive engagement with industry updates in order to stay current with algorithm modifications. For the purpose of gathering information, main sources include official announcements made on social media sites. Participating in online forums, as well as subscribing to industry blogs and newsletters, enables one to gain deeper insights and engage in conversations around these changes. Your ability to predict shifts in algorithms and adjust your strategy accordingly is directly correlated to your level of awareness.

2. Perform an Analysis of the Data and Insights:

When navigating the ever-changing realm of social media algorithms, data serves as your compass. The performance of your material can be better understood by monitoring analytics on a regular basis, which provides significant insights. There are tangible indicators that can be used to determine how algorithms effect your exposure and audience involvement, and some examples of these metrics include reach, engagement, and click-through rates. The analysis of these data points gives you the ability to improve your approach and optimize your content in order to achieve better results from the algorithm.

3. Assess and Make Adjustments:

To stay one step ahead of algorithmic advances, experimentation is absolutely necessary. Through the process of testing various content formats, posting times, and techniques, you are able to determine what resonates most strongly with your audience and is in line with the preferences indicated by algorithms. Continuous experimentation enables incremental refining of your strategy, which ensures relevance in a digital ecosystem that is constantly evolving. This can be accomplished by playing around with the frequency of your posts or by adjusting the visual aspects.

(4) Put an emphasis on quality rather than quantity:

It is more important to prioritize quality over quantity when it comes to algorithmic favor! Promoting meaningful engagement and increasing the possibility of algorithmic prioritizing are both outcomes that can be achieved by giving priority to high-quality content. Your goal should be to produce material that enhances the experience of your audience, thereby generating genuine interactions and opportunities for sharing. The cultivation of brand reputation and loyalty is facilitated by quality content, which not only withstands the inspection of algorithmic systems.

5. Encourage Activity and Participation:

The algorithms that power social media platforms are dependent on engagement. Increasing the visibility and reach of your content can be accomplished by actively connecting with your audience and encouraging community participation. For the purpose of fostering interaction and expanding relationships, it is beneficial to encourage likes, comments, shares, and user-generated material. When you spark conversation by asking questions and provoking discussions, you are sending a signal to algorithms about the relevancy and resonance of the information you are producing.

Diversify your content strategy, which is number six:

The impact of algorithmic adjustments on any one platform can be mitigated by diversifying the content approach that is used. Utilize a multi-format strategy, which includes the incorporation of photographs, videos, tales, and live broadcasts, in order to respond to the tastes of a wide audience. Increasing your presence across various social media platforms not only broadens your audience but also lessens your dependency on the algorithmic whims of a single network. The cultivation of resilience in the face of algorithmic uncertainty can be accomplished through the diversification of your presence.

Keep your flexibility and be able to quickly adapt:

When it comes to negotiating the constantly altering terrain of social media algorithms, agility is of the utmost importance. Because trends emerge quickly and algorithms evolve quickly, it is necessary to make adjustments as soon as possible. Maintaining your relevance and visibility requires that you keep an eye on the activities of your competitors, recognize any new trends that emerge, and change your strategy accordingly. Accept change as a chance for growth and commit to consistently refining your approach in order to stay ahead of the curve when it comes to algorithm innovation.

In conclusion, in order to successfully navigate algorithm changes and trends, one must employ a comprehensive approach that incorporates awareness, analysis, experimentation, and adaptability. It is possible to successfully manage the complexities of social media algorithms if you maintain a high level of awareness, make use of data insights, and place a high priority on producing quality engagement. In order to position yourself for sustained success in the ever-changing world of social media, you need open yourself up to change and view it as a chance for creativity and progress.

Chapter 8: Building a Strong Personal Brand

In this day and age, where social media controls the majority of our contacts on a daily basis, it is very necessary to develop a powerful personal brand in order to achieve success. A well-defined personal brand acts as a beacon, encouraging people to connect with your own personality, beliefs, and products. This is especially important in spite of the noise and rivalry that exists in the market. In order to create a captivating personal brand on social media, let's go deeper into the steps that are essential to the process.

In the first place, define your brand identity:

A distinct and unmistakable personality is the vital component that underpins the success of any personal brand. To get started, you need engage in some self-reflection and determine what differentiates you from other people operating in your specialized field. Think about the qualities that make up your persona, such as your strengths, interests, and values. This self-awareness will serve as the basis upon which you will construct the personality and voice of your brand. Keep in mind that authenticity is of the utmost importance; the identity of your brand should be compatible with the people you are trying to reach.

2. Share your personal narrative:

Every single personal brand is made up of a story that is just ready to be told. Your experiences, achievements, and failures, along with your path, all come together to produce a story that is very captivating. Authenticity and honesty are two qualities that you should embrace when you are sharing your story with your audience. Through the use of narrative, you can humanize your brand, which will allow you to develop emotional connections and establish relatability, which will in turn foster greater engagement and loyalty among your followers.

3. **The Importance of Consistency:**

In order to keep your personal brand cohesive throughout all of the different social media channels, consistency is quite important. Make sure that your brand identity, messaging, and visual aspects are consistent with one another. Maintaining a consistent brand experience that resonates with your audience is essential, and this includes everything from the colors and typefaces to the tone of voice and imagery. The cultivation of familiarity and trust, two crucial components for the development of a powerful and easily recognizable brand presence, is fostered by consistency.

(4) Offer Something of Value:

Making a commitment to offering value to your audience is essential to the success of any personal brand. Your followers will appreciate it if you share insightful content, relevant insights, and your knowledge that addresses their needs and interests. Take the initiative to establish oneself as a reliable source of information and motivation within your specialized field. By delivering value on a constant basis, you develop credibility and authority, which in turn attracts and keeps a loyal following that is eager to engage with your brand.

5. Interact with the People in Your Audience:

Developing a personal brand is not a one-way street; rather, it is about cultivating meaningful connections and interactions with the people who come into contact with your brand. You should answer to comments, messages, and mentions from your followers in order to actively engage with them. Fostering a sense of community and belonging can be accomplished by starting conversations, asking questions, and soliciting opinions from others. Authentic involvement helps to establish rapport with your audience and strengthens the connection that you share with them.

Authenticity and transparency are the sixth point.

Because we live in a society that is overflowing with curated content and polished identities, authenticity stands out as a guiding light for that which is genuine. In order to demonstrate to your audience that you are your own self, you should embrace your peculiarities, foibles, and oddities. Providing your followers with transparency helps to establish trust, which in turn encourages deeper ties and loyalty. You should always be true to your views and ideals, and you should always allow your authentic personality to shine through in every conversation.

7. Invest in Your Brand:

You are making an investment in your future success when you make an investment in your personal brand. It is important to allocate resources to the creation of high-quality content, professional branding, and graphic assets that accurately reflect the essence of your business. If you want to improve your abilities and expertise in your field, you might want to think about enrolling in classes, getting coaching, or finding a mentor. It is important to keep in mind that every investment you make in the expansion of your brand will pay off in the form of a powerful and influential presence on social media.

Eighth, Remain Unwavering in Your Obligations:

When you are working to establish a personal brand, it is imperative that you do not lose sight of your fundamental ideals and values. Your brand need to be a genuine reflection of who you are and what you believe in. The temptation to compromise your integrity for the sake of popularity or validation is something you should fight against. You can create trust and credibility by remaining true to your ideals, which will, in the long term, lay the framework for ongoing success and impact.

In conclusion, in order to construct a powerful personal brand on social media, it is necessary to employ a smart combination of components such as authenticity, consistency, value, and interaction. You are able to create a brand that deeply resonates with your audience and distinguishes you from the competition in a crowded digital landscape by defining your brand identity, sharing your story, providing value, engaging with your audience, being authentic and transparent, investing in your brand, and remaining true to your values. That being said, you should celebrate your individuality, tell your narrative, and allow your personal brand to shine brilliantly for the rest of the world to witness.

Chapter 9: Collaborating with Influencers and Partners

In the current digital environment, influencer marketing has evolved as a powerful tactic for organizations that are looking to broaden their audience reach, interact with new demographics, and increase conversions on social media platforms. Brands have the ability to tap into established audiences, utilize the credibility and authority of prominent voices, and magnify their brand messaging in a manner that is both authentic and impactful when they forge relationships with strategic partners and influencers. This chapter not only elucidates the complexities of effective collaboration with influencers and partners on social media, but it also outlines a thorough strategy for maximizing the benefits that may be gained from such engagements.

The first step is to identify the appropriate influencers:
The careful selection of the appropriate influencers is the most important factor in the success of influencer collaborations. Having a nuanced understanding of the values of the brand, the demographics of the target audience, and the goals of the campaign is required for this. Influencers whose material is in

perfect harmony with the niche or industry in which they operate should be sought out by brands in order to cultivate a genuine rapport with their following. When analyzing possible collaborators, metrics such as engagement rates, audience demographics, and content quality serve as crucial yardsticks. This helps to ensure that the potential collaborators are aligned with the ideology of the brand and the communication goals that it has set.

Establishing and Maintaining Relationships:

In order for influencer collaborations to be successful, it is essential to cultivate genuine relationships with the individuals involved. Engaging with influencers across social media platforms and displaying genuine interest in their content and initiatives is something that brands should make an effort to do, investing both time and effort in the process. Personalized outreach, which is marked by real admiration and targeted collaboration proposals, creates the framework for long-lasting partnerships that are built on mutual respect and confidence.

Clearly defining your goals is the next step.
Before beginning any endeavors that include collaboration, it is of the utmost importance to establish crystal-clear objectives

and measurable goals for the relationship. Whether the objective is to increase sales, increase website traffic, or increase brand awareness, it is of the utmost importance to have a clear understanding of the desired outcomes. In order to assist the systematic evaluation of the efficacy of collaboration, the establishment of key performance indicators (KPIs) is necessary. This allows stakeholders to monitor progress and modify tactics in accordance with the measured outcomes.

Fourth, the process of co-creating compelling content:

The co-creation of captivating content that resonates with the influencer's audience while simultaneously supporting the brand message is the most important aspect of successful influencer collaborations. It is important for brands to provide creative autonomy to influencers while also providing guidance to ensure that their creativity aligns with the values of the brand and the goals of the campaign. Whether it be through sponsored posts, product reviews, or collaborations on branded content, the focus should be on providing value to the audience of the influencer as well as the audience of the business.

Regarding the Disclosure of Sponsored Content:

Influencer marketing strategies that adhere to ethical standards are built on the foundation of transparency and sincerity. When it comes to compliance with relevant legislation and guidelines, brands have a responsibility to ensure that sponsored content is disclosed in a clear and visible manner. Transparent and trustworthy relationships with the audience are fostered by the use of clear signs such as the hashtags #ad or #sponsored to indicate paid collaborations. Fostering an environment in which influencers are encouraged to openly reveal their ties helps to strengthen the integrity of brand-influencer partnerships.

6. Taking Measurements and Making Adjustments:

For the purpose of determining whether or not influencer collaborations are successful, it is essential to conduct meticulous monitoring and analysis. Through the utilization of analytics and tracking technologies, stakeholders are able to evaluate performance in relation to important metrics like as reach, engagement, and conversions. An informed decision-making process is made possible by the insights that are gathered from performance data. This enables businesses to improve their strategies and refine their future collaborations in order to achieve greater efficacy.

Assisting in the Maintenance of Long-Term Relationships:

When it comes to the field of influencer marketing, making an investment in the cultivation of long-term relationships with partners and influencers delivers a multitude of returns. It is important for brands to take the initiative to cultivate these connections by providing continuing assistance, chances for cooperation, and value exchanges that are mutually beneficial. Fostering a sense of partnership and solidarity, which is the foundation for long-lasting collaborations that are founded on mutual benefit, can be accomplished by expressing gratitude for the contributions made by the influencer and celebrating the victories that have been achieved together.

In conclusion, in order to collaborate with influencers and partners on social media in an efficient manner, it is necessary to take a comprehensive approach that includes careful influencer screening, relationship development, goal alignment, content co-creation, transparency, performance measurement, and relationship nurturing. Amplifying their presence, cultivating genuine connections with their target audience, and accomplishing their marketing goals on social media platforms are all things that brands can accomplish by embracing the power of influencer marketing and utilizing the impact of trusted voices.

Chapter 10: Analyzing Metrics and Data for Success

In the current fast-paced digital landscape, social media has evolved into a powerful tool that individuals and organizations alike can use to interact with their audience, increase brand exposure, and generate engagement. On the other hand, in order to successfully traverse this changing environment, one must learn to harness the power of data. When it comes to knowing the performance of your social media efforts and making decisions that are informed in order to optimize your plan for success, analyzing metrics and data is not just a task; it is a key component of comprehending the effectiveness of your efforts. As we progress through this chapter, we will delve deeply into the process of assessing metrics and statistics for success on social media. We will also investigate essential strategies and approaches that will allow you to maximize your influence.

1. Define Your Goals and Key Performance Indicators:
To ensure that your social media strategy is successful, it is essential to first set crystal defined objectives and key performance indicators (KPIs) before beginning any kind of data analysis. In order to serve as guiding principles for your data analysis activities, these objectives ought to be SMART,

which stands for specified, measurable, attainable, relevant, and time-bound. Establishing specific objectives can provide a framework for measuring the effectiveness of your social media initiatives. Whether your objective is to enhance brand awareness, generate visitors to your website, or boost engagement, having clear objectives will provide you with a framework.

2. **Keep an eye on metric that is pertinent:**

Given the abundance of metrics that are available, it is of the utmost importance to concentrate on those measures that are in accordance with your goals and offer insightful information regarding your performance. The efficacy of your social media presence can be evaluated using measures like as reach, engagement (including likes, comments, and shares), click-through rates, conversion rates, follower growth, and post-performance analytics. By monitoring these data on a consistent basis, you will be able to get useful insights into the behavior of your audience as well as the performance of your material, which will allow you to adjust your strategy accordingly.

Utilize the Tools for Analytical Use:

There is a plethora of analytics tools available on social media platforms, which provide essential data and insights into audience demographics, content performance, interaction trends, and other related topics. By utilizing technologies such as Facebook Insights, Twitter Analytics, Instagram Insights, LinkedIn Analytics, and YouTube Analytics, you may have extensive visibility into the performance of your social media accounts. Through the efficient utilization of these tools, you will be able to monitor progress, recognize trends, and evaluate the repercussions of your efforts throughout the course of time.

4. Establishing a Benchmark Against Competitors

An analysis of the social media performance of rivals provides significant benchmarking insights as well as chances for improvement. You are able to find competitive advantages and places for difference by comparing your performance metrics, audience demographics, content strategy, and engagement levels with those of your competitors. The context that this comparison study gives is extremely helpful for evaluating your own performance and determining methods that will allow you to outperform competitors in your preferred field.

5. **Divide Your Audience Into Segments:**

In order to adjust your content and approach to the tastes and interests of your audience, it is essential to have a solid understanding of your target. You will be able to obtain a more in-depth understanding of your audience's preferences, requirements, and behaviors if you segment them according to demographics, psychographics, behavior, and engagement levels. You will be able to maximize engagement and promote meaningful interactions with your business if you create content that is specifically targeted to different audience segments and create personalized experiences for those audience segments.

Identifying the Content That Is Performing the Best:

It is crucial to conduct an analysis of material that is performing exceptionally well in order to find patterns, trends, and themes that resonate with your audience. Discovering insights into what generates engagement and resonates with your audience may be accomplished by analyzing many aspects of the material, including the format, topic, timing, images, and messaging for the content. By utilizing these insights, you will be able to reproduce material that has been effective and refine your content strategy to get the most possible impact.

Seventh, iterate and make improvements:

The analysis of data is a process that is iterative and requires ongoing monitoring, testing, and improvement during the process. You will be able to generate continual optimization and success if you use the insights gathered from your analysis to inform future decisions and adjustments to your social media strategy. Adapting to shifting tastes and trends is made possible by the process of experimenting with new strategies and tactics, measuring the effectiveness of those strategies, and iterating depending on the insights gained from data. This helps to ensure that your approach continues to be effective over time.

As a conclusion, it is essential to conduct measurements and data analysis in order to achieve success in the always developing universe of social media. You are able to optimize your social media strategy for maximum impact and achieve meaningful results by establishing clear objectives and key performance indicators (KPIs), tracking relevant metrics, utilizing analytics tools, benchmarking against competitors, segmenting your audience, identifying top-performing content, and iterating based on data-driven insights. Now is the time to pull up your sleeves, get into your analytics, and allow data to serve as your guide to achieving success on social media.

Chapter 11: Handling Negative Feedback and Crisis Management

In today's digitally-driven world, when social media serves as both a platform for promotion and a breeding ground for criticism, mastering the ability to navigate negative comments and crisis situations has become a crucial talent for organizations. The manner in which you respond to these difficult situations can have a big impact on the integrity and reputation of your brand. In the following chapter, we will discuss successful ways for managing negative comments and crises on social media. We will place an emphasis on proactive measures, clear communication, and a dedication to transparency and accountability.

To begin, keep an eye on the comments and mentions:
Maintaining vigilance and keeping track of mentions of your business, product, or service across a variety of social media platforms is one of the fundamental elements included in the process of handling negative criticism on social media. Monitoring comments, reviews, and direct messages is an important part of this process since it allows you to detect any problems or critiques that have been made by your audience. Keeping yourself updated allows you to intervene in a timely

manner to address concerns before they become more serious, which demonstrates your commitment to ensuring that your customers are totally satisfied.

2. Respond in a prompt and professional manner:

In situations where one is confronted with unfavorable feedback or criticism on social media, the urge to ignore or remove it can be quite powerful. On the other hand, this strategy may not only fail but also cause more harm to the reputation of your brand. Rather than that, you should answer in a fast and professional manner, noting the concerns that were voiced and offering empathy and understanding. In situations where it is appropriate to do so, a genuine apology can go a long way toward defusing emotions and displaying your dedication to finding a solution to the problem.

3. Engage in Conversations While You Are Offline:

Depending on the circumstances, public forums might not be the most suitable settings for addressing issues that are particularly delicate or complicated. In situations like these, it is recommended to take conversations offline in order to resolve issues in a manner that is both private and effective. Individuals should be provided with contact information or directed to established customer service channels in order to provide them the opportunity to have their concerns addressed in further detail. You will not only be able to safeguard the privacy of the individual, but you will also be able to maintain a professional image on social media for yourself.

4. Maintain Your Professionalism and Calmness:
While it is important to have a level head and act in a professional manner while interacting with others on social media, it is also important to remember that negative feedback and criticism can provoke powerful emotional responses. It is important to avoid getting involved in heated discussions or exchanging insults with those who are critical of your brand because doing so might make the situation even worse and reflect poorly on your brand. Your attention should instead be directed toward finding a solution that satisfies the customer and resolving the problem in a constructive manner.

5. Ensure that there is transparency and regular updates:
The need of transparency cannot be overstated, especially in times of crisis. You should make sure that your audience is kept informed and up to date on the situation, including the actions that you are taking to remedy the problem and prevent it from happening again. Regardless of whether or not the facts reflect badly on your brand, you should always be honest and forthright about them. Transparency helps to develop trust and credibility, which in turn helps to reduce the negative impact

that the crisis has on the reputation of your brand.

6. **Empower Your workforce**: In order to effectively manage bad criticism and crises on social media, it is necessary to have a workforce that is both well-equipped and empowered. Your social media staff should be provided with clear instructions, protocols, and training in order to enable them to respond to consumer problems in a quick, professional, and compassionate manner. To guarantee that your team is able to respond to crises in a coordinated and cohesive manner, you should cultivate a culture of open communication and collaboration within your team.

7. **Acquire Knowledge and Experiment**:
Your company can benefit greatly from the various learning opportunities that are presented by negative feedback and crisis situations. It is important to do post-mortem assessments in order to analyze how the scenario was handled, identify any gaps or flaws in your reaction, and put remedial measures into place in order to prevent similar instances from occurring in the future. The ability to grow stronger and more resilient as a result of learning from previous experiences enables one to be better prepared to deal with challenges in the future.

The conclusion is that in order to effectively manage bad comments and crisis situations on social media, you need to have a proactive mindset, a commitment to customer happiness, and a determination to protecting the reputation of your company with honesty and transparency. Monitoring mentions and comments, responding in a prompt and professional manner, taking conversations offline when it is necessary, maintaining composure and professionalism, providing transparency and updates, empowering your team, and learning and improving from previous experiences are all ways in which you can successfully navigate these challenges and emerge stronger as a brand.

Chapter 12: Fostering Community and Building Brand Advocacy

inside the context of the interconnected digital landscape of today, social media has evolved into an essential component for companies that are looking to create a devoted community of followers and supporters inside their brand. Within the context of social media platforms, this chapter delves into the techniques and methods that are particularly important for cultivating communities and constructing brand advocacy.

Create Shared Spaces

Establishing dedicated venues on social media platforms where your audience can congregate, interact, and engage with your brand is essential for the development of a sense of community and belonging among your audience. It is possible for these spaces to take the shape of Facebook Groups, LinkedIn Communities, Twitter Chats, or Instagram hashtags. These spaces offer forums for individuals who have similar interests to communicate with one another, seek advice from one another, and encourage one another.

Ensure that meaningful conversations are facilitated.

For the purpose of establishing solid relationships and cultivating brand loyalty, it is essential to encourage meaningful interactions within your community. Participate actively in the interaction with your audience by posing questions, requesting feedback, and initiating conversations on issues that are pertinent to your brand and the industry. Establishing an atmosphere that is conducive to the growth of genuine talks can be accomplished by demonstrating a genuine interest in the thoughts and experiences of the other person.

Recognize and reward participation in activities.

Recognizing and recognizing individuals of the community who are actively engaged with your business is an essential step in the process of cultivating brand advocacy. Present content that was developed by users, emphasize testimonials from satisfied customers, and promote members of the community who exemplify the principles of your company. By providing additional incentives, awards, or unique privileges, participants are further encouraged to prolong their involvement and participation, which in turn helps to cultivate a sense of gratitude and belonging within the community.

Enable Your Community to Take Action

It is possible to amplify the message of your brand and encourage organic growth by providing your community members with the ability to become advocates for your brand. Ensure that they have access to the tools, resources, and assistance they require in order to allow them to share their enthusiasm for your business with others. In order to enable your community to become brand ambassadors, you should encourage user-generated content, supply assets that can be shared, and offer possibilities for cooperation on campaigns or initiatives.

Listen and give your response.

By actively listening to the views, recommendations, and concerns of your community, you are demonstrating that you appreciate their input and are devoted to satisfying their needs. You should respond in a fast and transparent manner, addressing their comments and implementing it into your product development, marketing plans, and customer service methods. Building trust and loyalty among members of your community can be accomplished by demonstrating that you are attentive to their requirements.

Content that adds value should be created.

It is crucial to provide material that is both meaningful and relevant, particularly content that is suited to the interests of your community, in order to drive interaction and generate brand advocacy. It is important to provide educational tools, insights into the sector, and how-to guides that address the issues and goals of the employees. Establishing your brand as a reliable resource within the community may be accomplished by providing material that not only makes their life more enjoyable but also assists them in accomplishing their objectives.

"Set an Example for Others"

In order to establish trust and credibility, it is of the utmost importance to set an example for others to follow and to reflect the values of your brand in all of your interactions with the community. When you communicate with your audience, demonstrate that you are sincere in your commitment to developing meaningful relationships with them by being honest, transparent, and empathic. You may create trust, loyalty, and advocacy among the people of your community by exhibiting the personality and values of your company.

In conclusion, in order to cultivate a robust sense of community and to generate brand advocacy on social media, it is necessary to take a comprehensive approach that places an emphasis on participation, empowerment, and authenticity. You can cultivate a loyal community of brand advocates who will champion your brand and help drive its success by designing shared spaces, facilitating meaningful conversations, recognizing and rewarding engagement, empowering your community, listening to feedback and responding to it, creating content that adds value, and setting an example for others to follow. Because of this, you should make an investment in the development of your community, establish genuine relationships, and watch as the influence and impact of your business rise enormously.

Chapter 13: Embracing Diversity and Inclusion

It is not only a laudable desire for brands that want to succeed in a diverse marketplace to embrace diversity and inclusion in today's interconnected world, where social media serves as a strong instrument for communication and community-building. Rather, it is a strategic requirement for brands that want to thrive in a diverse marketplace. Brands have the ability to create an online community that is more accepting and supportive, and that reflects the vast tapestry of human experiences and opinions, by actively supporting diversity and cultivating an atmosphere that is inclusive. Together, we will investigate the ways in which brands may successfully embrace diversity and inclusion on social media.

1. **Celebrate Diversity:**

Recognizing and appreciating differences in racial and ethnic affiliation, gender, sexual orientation, age, ability, religious affiliation, and socioeconomic background is an essential component in embracing diversity. In order to celebrate diversity, you must incorporate a variety of viewpoints and experiences into the content, visuals, and narratives of your business. To develop a story that is more inclusive, it is important to showcase the tales of individuals who come from a variety of backgrounds and to highlight the distinctive contributions they have made.

2. Educate and advocate for the cause:

For the purpose of educating your audience about the significance of diversity and inclusion, as well as advocating for social justice and equality, social media gives a platform that can be utilized. In order to create awareness of issues relating to diversity, equity, and inclusion, it is important to share materials, articles, and stories among people. Raising awareness of the realities of oppressed people and advocating for positive change are two ways to amplify the voices of those communities.

3. Include a Wide Range of Voices:

You may amplify the voices of people who come from groups that are underrepresented or marginalized by include them in your content, collaborations, and initiatives. Make sure that your audience has the opportunity to hear from a wide range of creators, influencers, and thought leaders who are willing to offer their experiences, viewpoints, and areas of expertise. You are not only amplifying the voices of a broad group of people, but you are also giving them the ability to have a greater influence.

4. Establish Spaces That Are Inclusive:

Create a social media community that is welcoming, respectful, and valued for all users, and encourage them to feel respected and valued. Establish unambiguous principles and community standards that forbid any type of intolerance, including but not limited to hate speech, harassment, discrimination, and any other of these. It is important to actively manage your social media platforms in order to guarantee that they continue to be secure and welcoming environments in which all users may engage and participate.

(5) Pay Attention and Take Notes:

Participate in attentively listening to the experiences, viewpoints, and comments of persons who come from a variety of different backgrounds. Maintain a mindset that is receptive to learning and unlearning biases that may be present inside your brand or throughout your audience. It is important to have meaningful talks about diversity and inclusion, and to make an effort to comprehend the various perspectives and experiences that people have gone through. By utilizing your platform, you can elevate the voices of those who are disenfranchised and push for significant change.

Give your support to a variety of causes:

By lending your support to causes, organizations, and

initiatives that advocate for social justice, equality, and representation, you can demonstrate your dedication to diversity and inclusion. Your brand should be aligned with initiatives to enhance diversity and inclusion both within your community and on a larger scale. This can be accomplished through donations, sponsorships, or participation in campaigns. It is possible for you to make a discernible contribution to the advancement of these vital issues by utilizing the resources and influence that you possess.

7. **Make sure you are accountable to yourself:**

In order to promote diversity and inclusion both internally and publicly, you should hold yourself and your business accountable when doing so. The methods, rules, and content of your organization should be evaluated on a regular basis to ensure that they are inclusive and representative of a variety of perspectives. Be willing to admit that you made a mistake and to apologize for any harm that you may have caused. In order to demonstrate your dedication to continual development and accountability, you should take real steps to remedy the issue and prevent it from happening again.

In conclusion, promoting diversity and inclusion on social media is not just a moral imperative for brands, but it also provides them with a strategic benefit. Contributing to the development of a society that is more fair and inclusive can be accomplished by activities such as celebrating diversity, educating and campaigning for inclusion, highlighting varied voices, establishing spaces that are inclusive, listening and learning, supporting diverse causes, and holding yourself accountable. Make use of your platform to highlight the voices of a varied range of people, to challenge stereotypes, and to cultivate a culture that encourages acceptance and belonging for all individuals. By doing so, you not only improve the reputation of your brand, but you also have a significant impact on the world that is all around you.

Chapter 14: Harnessing the Power of Visual Storytelling

In today's digitally saturated market, when attention spans are short and competition for engagement is severe, it has become absolutely necessary for companies that want to differentiate themselves from their competitors and build meaningful connections with their audiences to become proficient in the art of visual storytelling. Because social media platforms place such a strong focus on attractive visuals and multimedia content, they offer a fertile field for businesses to build intriguing narratives that truly engage with their fans. This chapter will go into the strategies and tactics that can empower you to harness the transformative potential of visual storytelling on social media. These strategies and techniques can be found in this chapter.

1. Use High-Quality Visuals:
The foundation of high-quality images is the most important component of any visual storytelling endeavor that is achieved with success. It is vital to make investments in professional photography, videography, and graphic design in order to create visually arresting material that can stop the scrolling thumb of the modern social media user. An effective visual

narrative is built on well-defined, clear images that are infused with vivid colors and painstaking attention to detail. These images serve as the foundation of the narrative.

2. Recount a Story Through the Use of images:

The potential of images to communicate narratives that resonate on a visceral level and to transcend linguistic barriers is a natural ability that images possess. You can harness this power by weaving a unified story through your images. This tale should not only highlight the products and services that your company provides, but it should also embody the brand's ethos, values, and personality. Allow your imagery to function as a conduit for storytelling that captivates and engages your audience. This can be accomplished by highlighting user-generated content or providing behind-the-scenes peeks into the culture of your organization.

3. Evoke Emotion:

In every story that goes down in history, emotion is the driving force. Make use of the power of pictures to evoke a range of feelings that will resonate with your audience on a profound level. These feelings may include happiness, empathy, surprise, or nostalgia. You are able to develop stronger connections with your followers and make an impact that is long-lasting and extends beyond the sphere of digital media if you create images that strikes an emotional chord.

4. Establish a Visual Branding Strategy That Is Consistent:

When it comes to developing a powerful visual identity that resonates with your audience, consistency is the most important factor. You can not only strengthen the identity of your business by ensuring that your visual branding is consistent across all of your social media channels, but you can also ensure that your brand is instantly recognized amidst the sea of content that is competing for attention. Establishing a coherent brand narrative that makes an indelible impact on the awareness of your audience may be accomplished by utilizing colors, typefaces, and visual elements that are consistent with one another.

Experiment with a variety of different formats:

Diversity is the spice of life, and it is also the key to maintaining the interest of your audience. Explore a wide variety of visual formats, such as photographs, movies, carousels, narratives, and live streams, in order to accommodate a wide range of interests and patterns of consumption. You are able to maintain the freshness, vitality, and relevance of your content in the ever-changing environment of social media by consistently inventing and adapting to current trends.

Sixth, incorporate content that was generated by users:

It is possible to provide your audience the ability to become co-creators of the tale of your brand by soliciting and displaying content that was made by users. Not only does user-generated content add authenticity and credibility to your brand, but it also develops a sense of community and belonging among your followers. This is true whether the content in question is customer testimonials, product evaluations, or creative interpretations of your brand.

Seventh, optimize for mobile devices:

Because of the rise of mobile devices, optimizing your visual content for consumption on mobile devices is no longer in the realm of possibility; rather, it is an absolute need. You should make sure that your photos and videos are optimized for speedy loading and seamless viewing on a variety of screen sizes, and you should embrace mobile-friendly formats such as square or vertical movies. It is possible to provide a frictionless user experience that maximizes engagement and retention by giving mobile optimization the level of priority it deserves.

Eighth, Share Your Stories Across Multiple Platforms:

Each social media site has its own ecosystem and audience demographics that are distinct from those of other platforms. Make sure that your visual storytelling efforts are tailored to the specific qualities and preferences of each platform, while at the same time ensuring that your visual style and messaging are consistent across all platforms. Increasing your reach, cultivating brand loyalty, and developing a unified brand presence that extends beyond individual platforms are all possible outcomes that may be achieved by extending your narrative across various channels.

As a conclusion, visual storytelling is a powerful tool that can be utilized by organizations that are looking to differentiate themselves from the overwhelming amount of digital noise, establish meaningful connections with their audience, and enhance their presence on social media. Through the utilization of high-quality visuals, the creation of compelling narratives, the evocation of emotion, the maintenance of consistent branding, the experimentation with diverse formats, the incorporation of user-generated content, the optimization for mobile, and the adoption of cross-platform storytelling, you can unlock the full potential of visual storytelling and propel your brand to unprecedented heights of success. Now is the time to let your imagination run wild and embark on a visual voyage that will captivate not only your heart but also your mind and your screen.

Chapter 15: Embracing the Future of Social Media

The landscape of social media continues to evolve at a pace that has never been seen before in this era of rapid technology advancement and ever-changing user habits. As a result of developments such as the proliferation of artificial intelligence and the introduction of new platforms and formats, the future of social media holds a tremendous amount of promise for individuals who are prepared to adapt, create, and welcome change. As we progress through this chapter, we will delve deeper into the ways in which you can prepare for the future of social media by staying ahead of trends, embracing new platforms, adapting to changing algorithms, prioritizing authenticity and transparency, investing in relationships, prioritizing personalization, being prepared for crises, and remaining compliant with regulations.

1. **Stay Ahead of Trends:**

Maintaining a current awareness of the evolving trends and technologies that are transforming the digital landscape is very necessary in order to be successful in the future of social media. It is important to keep a close eye on the latest advances in cutting-edge technologies such as artificial intelligence, virtual reality, augmented reality, live streaming, and other similar areas. In addition to creating new chances for companies to connect with their audience in ways that are more relevant and immersive, these developments have the potential to transform the way consumers interact and engage on social platforms.

2. **Embrace New Platforms**:

Maintain a mindset that is open to experimentation and exploration as new social media platforms and features continue to gain popularity. You should be proactive in evaluating and integrating these new prospects into your social media strategy. This applies whether it is a video-sharing app that is experiencing rapid growth, a community platform that caters to a certain niche, or a novel content type. Diversifying your presence across a number of different platforms allows you to reach new audiences and maintain a competitive advantage in a digital landscape that is constantly shifting and developing.

3. **Accommodate Algorithms That Are Still Changing:**

The algorithms that make up social media platforms are always being updated, which means that they can have an effect on how visible and accessible your content is. It is crucial to maintain agility and adjust your strategy in response to changes in algorithmic requirements if you wish to continue to be competitive. Through the utilization of data and insights, you can improve your content and maximize its impact, so ensuring that your brand continues to be visible and relevant despite the constant transformation of digital algorithms.

4. Place an emphasis on being genuine and being openly honest:

For brands that want to establish trust and credibility with their target audience in this day and age of increased skepticism and scrutiny, authenticity and transparency have become of the utmost importance. You can humanize your brand and establish genuine connections with your audience by sharing genuine tales, looks behind the scenes, and real-time updates throughout your social media accounts. You will be able to create a devoted community of followers who are in agreement with the values and mission of your business if you make honesty and transparency the top priorities in your communications.

5. Make an investment in your relationships:

The essence of social media lies in the process of establishing relationships with the people who follow you. You should devote some of your time and resources to cultivating these relationships by actively engaging with your followers, replying to their comments and messages, and giving value through the content you share and the conversations you have with them. You will be able to cultivate genuine connections that go beyond the domain of digital media and develop long-term loyalty and support for your business if you build a community of brand advocates who are loyal to your brand.

6. Make Personalization Your Number One Priority:
Personalization will become an essential distinction for organizations that are looking to stand out in the digital crowd as social media platforms continue to grow more saturated and competitive. offering personalized experiences that resonate on a deeper level can be accomplished by utilizing data and analytics to adjust your content and messaging to the specific tastes and interests of your audience for the purpose of offering personalized experiences. When you give personalization a higher priority, you may generate interactions that are more meaningful to your audience, which will in turn drive higher levels of engagement and conversion overall.

Seventh, Always Be Ready for an Emergency:
Even if social media brings a plethora of opportunities for brands, it also comes with a number of inherent hazards, such as the possibility of crises and unfavorable press. It is

important to take the initiative to build a complete plan for crisis management, to train your team to respond successfully to emergencies, and to keep the lines of communication open with your audience. You will be able to limit potential damage to your brand reputation and navigate tumultuous waters with resilience and professionalism if you are prepared for crises and follow through with your preparations.

8. Maintain Compliance:

It is crucial for brands to remain compliant with key laws and rules in order to remain in compliance with the regulations that govern social media, which are always evolving. Maintain a level of awareness regarding the modifications that may occur in the legislation governing data privacy, advertising standards, and content moderation policies. This will ensure that your social media practices are in accordance with the legal requirements. By putting compliance at the forefront of your priorities, you can reduce the likelihood of facing legal consequences and earn the audience's trust by displaying your dedication to ethical and responsible behavior.

In conclusion, the future of social media has a tremendous amount of promise for brands that are prepared to accept change, continue to innovate, and exploit new chances. You can position your brand for success in the dynamic and ever-changing landscape of social media by staying ahead of trends, embracing new platforms, adapting to changing algorithms, prioritizing authenticity and transparency, investing in relationships, prioritizing personalization, being prepared for crises, and remaining compliant with regulations. These are all ways to position your brand for success. For this reason, it is important to be open to change, maintain a flexible mindset, and make effective use of the power of social media in order to cultivate long-lasting brand loyalty.